AS YOU THINK

AS YOU THINK

by
James Allen

Edited and with an Introduction by
Marc Allen

Whatever Publishing, Inc.
San Rafael, California

This edited version © 1987 Marc Allen
Published by Whatever Publishing, Inc.
58 Paul Drive, San Rafael, CA 94903

87 88 89 90   5 4 3 2 1

Cover design and art direction by
Kathleen Vande Kieft
Cover background art by Mark Busacca
Text design by Nancy Benedict
Typesetting by Harrington-Young Typography
All rights reserved
ISBN 0-931432-46-4

Mind is the master power that molds and makes,
And we are Mind, and evermore we take,
The tool of thought, and shaping what we will,
Bring forth a thousand joys, a thousand ills.
We think in secret, and it comes to pass—
Environment is but our looking glass.

—James Allen

CONTENTS

Whatever you can do, or dream you can, begin it—
Boldness has genius, power, and magic in it.
—Goethe

INTRODUCTION

There has to be some power and some magic in a book that has been in print and selling successfully for nearly a hundred years. *As You Think* has proven to be one of the world's most enduring and best "self-help" books, in the best sense of the term. "Self-development" is a better term—or "self-empowerment." This little book can show us the greatness we are capable of, and give us the tools to achieve it.

The truth can always be stated simply. And when it is stated, it can have a deeply moving effect. It can change our lives, in fact. The truth can literally make us free, free from the limitations we have imposed upon ourselves. James Allen shows us so clearly that the key to our own personal power is in our minds, and he shows us how to use that key to unlock the greatest success and power we can imagine.

I discovered *As You Think* about seven years ago, when a friend gave me a cassette tape of Leonard Orr reading the book. I must have played that tape over a hundred times, while driving in my car, before I wore the tape out. Then I bought the book, and made a cassette copy in my own voice. I still listen, on occasion, when I feel a need for inspiration. After listening so many times, I've memorized large parts of it.

As these simple yet brilliantly shining words of James Allen have seeped slowly into my subconscious, supported by the repetition of a great many listenings and readings, my life has slowly and steadily changed for the better. I have ceased doing the things I don't want to do in life; I spend my time doing what I love. I have written successful books and recorded albums of my music. I have created, with the assistance of a great many wonderful people, a successful business which runs smoothly and supports me and many others abundantly. I have discovered my purpose in life, and I am steadily working to help create, in my own way, a better world for all of us.

The words of James Allen (who is no relation to me, incidentally) have definitely been a powerful guiding force in my life, and I am pleased and excited to be able to share them with you.

I have edited the book only slightly, changing language that has at times become dated or obsolete. The original title is *As A Man Thinketh*. Of course, the author meant women as well as men—as he writes in the opening of the book—for the principles he points out to us so clearly are universal, applying to everyone regardless of sex, age, race, beliefs, social standing, or education.

Enjoy the feast James Allen has prepared for you—a large, nourishing feast in a small package.

Marc Allen
Novato, California

FOREWORD

This little volume—the result of meditation and experience—is not intended as an exhaustive treatise on the much-written-upon subject of the power of thought. It is suggestive rather than explanatory, its object being to stimulate men and women to the discovery and perception of the truth that "they themselves are makers of themselves" by virtue of the thoughts which they choose and encourage; that mind is the master weaver, both of the inner garment of character and the outer garment of their circumstances and that, as they may have previously woven in ignorance and pain they may now weave in enlightenment and happiness.

James Allen
Ilfracombe, England

ONE

Thought
and
Character

The aphorism, "As we think in our hearts so are we," not only embraces the whole of our being, but it is so comprehensive as to reach out to every condition and circumstance of our lives. We are literally *what we think,* our character being the complete sum of all our thoughts.

As the plant springs from, and could not be without, the seed, so every one of our acts springs from the hidden seeds of our thoughts, and could not have appeared without them. This applies equally to those acts called "spontaneous" and "unpremeditated" as to those which are deliberately executed.

Act is the blossom of thought, and joy and suffering are its fruits; thus do we gather in the sweet and bitter fruits of our own planting.

What we are was designed and built by our own thoughts in our minds. If we nurture

ignorant or evil thoughts, pain will soon follow. If our thoughts are healthy and beneficial, joy will follow us as surely as our shadows follow us on a sunny day.

A man or a woman is a growth by law, not a creation by artifice, and such cause-and-effect is as absolute and undeviating in the hidden realm of thought as in the world of visible and material things. A noble and Godlike character is not a thing of favor or chance, but is the natural result of continued effort in right thinking, the effect of long-cherished association with Godlike thoughts. An ignoble and bestial character, by the same process, is the result of the continued harboring of grovelling thoughts.

We are made or unmade by ourselves; in the armory of thought we forge the weapons by which we destroy ourselves, and we also fashion the tools with which we build for ourselves heavenly mansions of joy and strength and peace. By the right choices and true applications of our thoughts, we ascend to divine perfection; by the abuses and wrong applications of our thoughts, we descend be-

low the level of the beast. Between these two extremes are all grades of character, and we are their makers and masters.

Of all the beautiful truths pertaining to the soul which have been restored and brought to light in this age, none is more gladdening or fruitful of divine promise and confidence than this—that you are the master of your thought, the molder of your character, and the maker and shaper of your condition, environment, and destiny.

As a being of power, intelligence, and love, and the lord of your own thoughts, you hold the key to every situation, and contain within yourself that transforming and regenerative agency by which you may make yourself what you will.

You are always the master, even in your weakest and most abandoned state; but in your weakness and degradation you are the foolish master who misgoverns your household. When you begin to reflect upon your condition, and to search diligently for the law upon which your being is established, you then become the wise master, directing

your energies with intelligence, and fashioning your thoughts to fruitful issues. Such is the *conscious* master, and you can only become a conscious master by discovering *within yourself* the laws of thought. This discovery is totally a matter of application, self-analysis, and experience.

Only by much searching and mining are gold and diamonds obtained, and you can find every truth connected with your being, if you will dig deep into the mine of your soul. The fact that you are the maker of your character, the molder of your life, and the builder of your destiny, you may unerringly prove, if you will watch, control, and alter your thoughts, tracing their effects upon yourself, upon others, and upon your life and circumstances, linking cause and effect by patient practice and investigation, and utilizing your every experience—even the most trivial, everyday occurrence—as a means of obtaining that knowledge of yourself which leads to understanding, wisdom, and power.

In this direction, as in no other, is the law absolute that "Those that seek shall find;

to those that knock the door shall be opened," for only by patience, practice, and ceaseless importunity can you enter the door of the temple of knowledge.

TWO

The Effect of
Thought on
Circumstances

Your mind may be likened to a garden, which may be intelligently cultivated or allowed to run wild—but whether cultivated or neglected, it must, and will, *bring forth*. If no useful seeds are put into it, then an abundance of useless weed seeds will fall therein, and will continue to produce their kind.

Just as gardeners cultivate their plots, keeping them free from weeds, and growing the flowers and fruits they desire, so may you tend the garden of your mind, weeding out all the wrong, useless, and impure thoughts, and cultivating toward perfection the flowers and fruits of right, useful, and pure thoughts. By pursuing this process, you will sooner or later discover that you are the master gardener of your soul, the director of your life. You also reveal, within yourself, the

laws of thought, and understand, with ever-increasing accuracy, how the forces of thought and elements of the mind operate in the shaping of your character, circumstances, and destiny.

Thought and character are one, and as character can only manifest and discover itself through environment and circumstance, the outer conditions of your life will always be found to be harmoniously related to your inner state. This does not mean that your circumstances at any given time are an indication of your *entire* character, but that those circumstances are so intimately connected with some vital element of your thought that, for the time being, they are indispensable to your development.

You are where you are by the law of your being; the thoughts which you have built into your character have brought you there, and in the arrangement of your life there is no element of chance, but all is the result of a law which cannot err. This is just as true of those who feel "out of harmony" with their surroundings as of those who are contented with them.

As a progressive and evolving being, you are where you are in order to learn and to grow, and as you learn the spiritual lesson which any circumstance contains for you, it passes away and gives place to other circumstances.

You are buffeted by circumstances so long as you believe yourself to be a creature affected by outside conditions—but when you realize that you are a creative power, and that you may command the hidden soil and seeds of your being out of which your circumstances grow, then you become the rightful master of yourself.

All people who have practiced self-examination and self-control know that circumstances grow out of thought, for they have noticed that the alterations in their circumstances have been in direct proportion to their altered mental conditions. So true is this that when you earnestly apply yourself to remedy the defects in your character, you make swift and marked progress and pass rapidly through a series of changes.

The soul attracts that which it secretly harbors—that which it loves, and also that

which it fears. It reaches the height of its cherished aspirations, and it falls to the depth of its recurring, unexamined fears. Circumstances are the means by which the soul receives its own.

Every thought-seed sown or allowed to fall into the mind, and to take root there, produces its own, blossoming sooner or later into act, and bearing its own fruits of opportunity and circumstance. Good thoughts bear good fruit, bad thoughts bear bad fruit.

The outer world of circumstance shapes itself to the inner world of thought, and both pleasant and unpleasant external conditions are factors which make for the ultimate good of the individual. As the reaper of your own harvest, you learn both by suffering and bliss.

Following the innermost desires, aspirations, thoughts, by which you allow yourself to be dominated, you at last arrive at their fruition and fulfillment in the outer conditions of your life. The laws of growth and adjustment apply everywhere.

A person does not end up in the gutter or a prison by the tyranny of fate or circumstance, but by the path of low thoughts and base desires. Nor does a pure-minded person fall suddenly into crime by the stress of any merely external force—the criminal thought had long been secretly fostered in the heart, and the hour of opportunity revealed its gathered power. Circumstance does not make the person, it reveals the person to himself or herself.

No such conditions can exist that lead us to descend into vice and its attendant sufferings apart from our own vicious inclinations, just as no such conditions can exist that lead us to ascend into virtue and success and its pure happiness without the continued cultivation of virtuous and successful aspirations. We, therefore, as the lords and masters of our thoughts, are the makers of ourselves, the shapers and authors of our environment.

Even at birth the soul comes to its own, and through every step of its earthly pilgrimage it attracts those combinations of conditions which reveal itself, which are the

reflections of its own purity and impurity, its strength and weakness.

We do not attract what we *want,* but what we *are.* Our whims, fancies, and ambitions are thwarted at every step, but our innermost thoughts and desires are fed with their own food, be it good or bad. The "divinity that shapes our ends" is in ourselves; it is our very self. And so we are held prisoners only by ourselves: our own thoughts and actions are the jailers of our fate—they imprison, if they are base; they are also the angels of freedom—they liberate, if they are noble.

We don't get what we wish and pray for, we get what we justly earn. Our wishes and prayers are only gratified and answered when they harmonize with our thoughts and actions.

In the light of this truth, what then is the meaning of "fighting against circumstances" in our lives? It means that we are continually revolting against an *effect* without, while all the time we are nourishing and preserving its *cause* in our hearts. That

cause may take the form of a conscious vice or an unconscious weakness; but whatever it is, it stubbornly retards the efforts of its possessor, and calls aloud for a remedy.

Most of us are anxious to improve our circumstances, but are unwilling to improve ourselves—and we therefore remain bound. If we do not shrink from honest self-examination we can never fail to accomplish the object upon which our hearts are set. This is as true of earthly things as it is of heavenly things. Even if our sole object is to acquire wealth, we must be prepared to make great personal sacrifices before we can accomplish our object—and how much more so for those of us who would realize a strong and well-poised life?

Let's look at some examples:

Here are some people who are wretchedly poor. They are extremely anxious that their surroundings and home comforts should be improved, yet all the time they shirk their work, and consider they are justified in trying to deceive their employers on the grounds of the insufficiency of their

wages. These people do not understand the simple basic principles which are the basis of true prosperity, and are not only totally unfit to rise out of their poor condition, but are actually attracting to themselves still worse conditions by dwelling in—and acting out—weak, lazy, and deceptive thoughts.

Here is a rich couple who are the victims of a painful and persistent disease as the result of gluttony. They are willing to pay large sums of money to get rid of their illness, but they will not sacrifice their habits of overeating. They want to gratify their taste for rich foods in immoderate amounts and have their health as well. Such people are completely unfit for good health, because they have not yet learned the first principles of a healthy life.

Here are some employers of laborers who adopt crooked measures to avoid paying fair wages, and, in the hope of making larger profits, reduce the wages of their workpeople. These employers are altogether unfit for prosperity, and when they find themselves bankrupt, in both reputation and riches,

they blame circumstances, not knowing that they are the sole authors of their condition.

I have introduced these three cases merely to illustrate the truth that people are the causers—though nearly always unconsciously—of their circumstances, and that, while aiming at good ends, they are continually frustrating the accomplishment of those good ends by encouraging thoughts and desires which cannot possibly harmonize with those ends. Such cases could be multiplied and varied almost indefinitely, but this is not necessary, as we can, if we so resolve, trace the action of the laws of thought in our own mind and life—and until this is done, mere external facts cannot serve as a ground of reasoning.

Circumstances, however, are so complicated, thought is so deeply rooted, and the conditions of happiness vary so vastly with individuals, that our *entire* soul-condition (although it may be known to ourselves) cannot be judged by anyone else from the external aspects of our life alone. A person may be honest in certain directions, yet suf-

fer privations, while another person may be dishonest in certain directions, yet acquire wealth—but the conclusion usually formed that the one person fails *because of his or her particular honesty,* and that the other prospers *because of his or her particular dishonesty,* is the result of a superficial judgment, which assumes that the dishonest person is almost totally corrupt, and the honest person is almost entirely virtuous. In the light of a deeper knowledge and wider experience such judgment is found to be erroneous. The dishonest person may have some admirable virtues the other does not possess, and the honest person may have certain vices—even though subtle ones—which are absent in the other. The honest person reaps the good results of honest thoughts and acts, but also experiences the suffering that his or her vices produce. The dishonest person likewise garners his or her own suffering and happiness.

It is pleasing to human vanity to believe that one suffers because of one's virtue—but not until we have exterminated every sickly,

bitter, and impure thought from our mind, and washed every unhealthy stain from our soul, can we be in a position to know and declare that our sufferings are the result of our good, and not our bad qualities—and on the way to that supreme perfection, yet long before we have reached it, we will have found, working in our minds and our lives, a great law which is absolutely just, and which cannot, therefore, give good for evil, or evil for good. When we possess such knowledge, we will then know, as we look back upon our past ignorance and blindness, that our lives are, and always have been, justly ordered, and all our past experiences, good and bad, were the equitable outworkings of our evolving, yet unevolved self.

Good thoughts and actions can never produce bad results; bad thoughts and actions can never produce good results. This is but saying that nothing can come from corn but corn, nothing from nettles but nettles. We understand this law in the natural world, and work with it; but few understand it in the mental and moral world—although its oper-

ation there is just as simple and undeviating—and they, therefore, do not cooperate with it.

Suffering is *always* the effect of wrong thought in some direction. It is an indication that we are out of harmony with ourselves, with the law of our being. The sole and supreme use of suffering is to purify, to burn out all that is useless and impure. Suffering ceases for those who are pure. There can be no object in burning gold after the dross has been removed, and a perfectly pure and enlightened being cannot suffer.

The circumstances which we encounter with suffering are the result of our own mental inharmony. The circumstances we encounter with grace and pleasure are the result of our own mental harmony. Grace and pleasure, even blessedness—and not material possessions—are the measures of right thought; suffering and misery, not lack of material possessions, are the measures of wrong thought. Some people are miserable and rich; some are blessed and poor. Blessedness and riches are only joined together when the riches are rightly and wisely used;

and the poor only descend into misery when they regard their lot as a burden unjustly imposed upon them.

Poverty and over-indulgence are the two extremes of misery. They are both equally unnatural and both the result of mental disorder. We are not rightly conditioned until we are happy, healthy, and prosperous—and happiness, health, and prosperity are the result of a harmonious adjustment of the inner with the outer, of ourselves with our surroundings.

We only begin to be happy, healthy, and prosperous when we cease to whine and revile, and when we begin to search for the hidden justice which regulates our lives. And as we learn to adapt our minds to that regulating factor, we cease to accuse others as the cause of our condition, and we build ourselves up in strong and healthy thoughts; we cease to lash out against circumstances, and begin to *use* them as aids to our more rapid progress, and as a means of discovering the hidden powers and possibilities within ourselves.

Law, not confusion, is the dominating principle in the universe; justice, not injustice, is the soul and substance of life; and righteousness, not corruption, is the molding and moving force in the spiritual government of the world. This being so, we have to but right ourselves to find that the universe is right; and during the process of putting ourselves right, we will find that as we alter our thoughts towards things and other people, things and other people will alter towards us.

The proof of this truth is in every person, and it therefore admits of easy investigation by systematic introspection and self-analysis. Let us radically alter our thoughts, and we will be astonished at the rapid transformation it will effect in the material conditions of our lives. We imagine that our thought can be kept secret, but it cannot—it rapidly crystallizes into habit, and habit solidifies into circumstance.

Base thoughts crystallize into habits of drunkenness and resentment, which solidify into circumstances of destitution and suffering; destructive thoughts of every kind crys-

tallize into confusing and exhausting habits, which solidify into distracting and adverse circumstances; thoughts of fear, doubt, and indecision crystallize into weak and inconsistent habits, which solidify into circumstances of failure, poverty, and dependence; lazy thoughts crystallize into habits of uncleanliness and dishonesty, which solidify into circumstances of foulness and poverty; hateful and condemnatory thoughts crystallize into habits of accusation and violence, which solidify into circumstances of injury and persecution; selfish thoughts of all kinds crystallize into habits of self-seeking, which solidify into circumstances which are distressing.

On the other hand, beautiful thoughts of all kinds crystallize into habits of grace and kindliness, which solidify into genial and sunny circumstances; constructive thoughts crystallize into habits of temperance and self-control, which solidify into circumstances of repose and peace; thoughts of courage, self-reliance, and decision crystallize into strong and productive habits, which solidify into circumstances of success,

plenty, and freedom; energetic thoughts crystallize into habits of cleanliness and industry, which solidify into circumstances of pleasantness and pleasure; gentle and forgiving thoughts crystallize into habits of gentleness, which solidify into safe and healthy circumstances; loving and unselfish thoughts crystallize into habits of self-forgetfulness for others, which solidify into circumstances of sure and abiding prosperity and true riches.

A particular train of thought persisted in, be it good or bad, cannot fail to produce its results on our character and circumstances. We cannot *directly* choose our circumstances, but we can choose our thoughts, and so indirectly, yet surely, shape our circumstances.

Nature works with us and through us to help us gratify the thoughts we encourage the most, and opportunities are presented which will most speedily bring to the surface both the good and the destructive thoughts.

As soon as we cease from our negative and destructive thoughts, all the world softens toward us, and is ready to help us; as soon

as we put away our weak and sick thoughts, opportunities spring up on every hand to aid our strong resolve; as soon as we encourage good thoughts, no hard fate shall bind us down to misery and shame. The world is our kaleidoscope, and the varying combinations of colors which it presents to us at every succeeding moment are the exquisitely adjusted pictures of our ever-moving thoughts.

You will be what you will to be;
   Let failure find its false content
   In that poor word "environment",
But spirit scorns it, and is free.

It masters time, it conquers space,
   It cowes that boastful trickster, Chance,
   And bids the tyrant Circumstance
Uncrown, and take a servant's place.

The human Will, that force unseen,
   The offspring of a deathless Soul,
   Can hew a way to any goal,
Though walls of granite intervene.

Be not impatient in delay,
   But wait as one who understands;
   When spirit rises and commands,
The gods are ready to obey.

THREE

The Effect of Thought on Health and the Body

The body is the servant of the mind. It obeys the operations of the mind, whether they be deliberately chosen or automatically expressed. At the bidding of unhealthy thoughts the body sinks rapidly into disease and decay; at the command of glad and beautiful thoughts it becomes clothed with youthfulness and beauty.

Disease and health, like circumstances, are rooted in thought. Sickly thoughts will express themselves through a sickly body. Thoughts of fear have been known to kill a person as speedily as a bullet, and they are continually killing thousands of people just as surely, though less rapidly. The people who live in fear of disease are the people who get it. Anxiety quickly demoralizes the whole body, and lays it open to the entrance of disease; impure thoughts, even if not physically indulged, will soon shatter the nervous system.

Strong, pure, and happy thoughts build up the body in vigor and grace. The body is a delicate and plastic instrument, which responds readily to the thoughts by which it is impressed, and habits of thought will produce their own effects, good or bad, upon it.

People will continue to have impure and poisoned blood, so long as they propagate unclean thoughts. Out of a clean heart comes a clean life and a clean body. Out of a defiled mind proceeds a defiled life and an impure body. Thought is the source of action, life, and manifestation; make the source pure, and all will be pure.

A change of diet will not help those who will not change their thoughts. When our thoughts are pure, we no longer desire impure food.

Clean thoughts make clean habits. Those who have strengthened and purified their thoughts do not need to consider the malevolent microbe.

If you would perfect your body, guard your mind. If you would renew your body, beautify your mind. Thoughts of malice,

envy, disappointment, despondency, rob the body of its health and grace. A sour face does not come by chance; it is made by sour thoughts. Wrinkles that mar are drawn by folly, suffering, pride.

I know a woman of ninety-six who has the bright, innocent face of a girl. I know a man well under middle age whose face is drawn into inharmonious contours. The one is the result of a sunny disposition; the other is the outcome of suffering and discontent.

As you cannot have a sweet and wholesome place to live unless you admit the air and sunshine freely into your rooms, so a strong body and a bright, happy, or serene face can only result from the free admittance into the mind of thoughts of joy and goodwill and serenity.

On the faces of the aged there are wrinkles made by sympathy, others by strong and pure thought, and others are carved by negative emotions—who cannot distinguish them? For those who have lived righteously, age is calm, peaceful, and softly mellowed, like the setting sun. I recently saw a philoso-

pher on his deathbed. He was not old except in years. He died as sweetly and peacefully as he had lived.

There is no physician like cheerful thought for dissipating the ills of the body; there is no comforter to compare with good-will for dispersing the shadows of grief and sorrow. To live continually in thoughts of ill-will, cynicism, suspicion, and envy, is to be confined in a self-made prison cell. But to think well of all, to be cheerful with all, to patiently learn to find the good in all—such unselfish thoughts are the very portals of heaven, and to dwell day by day in thoughts of peace toward every creature will bring abounding peace to their possessor.

FOUR

Thought
and
Purpose

U ntil thought is linked with purpose there is no intelligent accomplishment. With most people, the bark of thought is allowed to drift upon the ocean of life. Aimlessness is a vice, and such drifting must not continue for those who would steer clear of catastrophe and destruction.

Those who have no central purpose in their lives fall an easy prey to petty worries, fears, troubles, and self-pityings, all of which are indications of weakness, and which lead, just as surely as deliberately planned crimes (though by a different route), to failure, unhappiness, and loss, for weakness cannot persist in a power-evolving universe.

We need to conceive of a legitimate purpose in our heart, and set out to accomplish it. We should make this purpose the centralizing point of our thoughts. It may take the form of a spiritual ideal, or it may be a

material object, according to our nature at the time; but whichever it is, we should steadily focus our thought-forces upon the object which we have set before ourselves. We should make this purpose our supreme duty, and devote ourselves to its attainment, not allowing our thoughts to wander away into ephemeral fancies, longings, and imaginings. This is the royal road to self-control and true concentration of thought. Even if we fail again and again to accomplish our purpose— as we necessarily must until our weakness is overcome—the *strength of character gained* will be the measure of our *true* success, and this will form a new starting point for future power and triumph.

Those who are not prepared for the apprehension of a *great* purpose should fix their thoughts upon the faultless performance of their duty, no matter how insignificant their task may appear. Only in this way can the thoughts be gathered and focused, and resolution and energy be developed, which being done, there is nothing which may not be accomplished.

The weakest soul, knowing its own weakness, and believing this truth—that *strength can only be developed by effort and practice*—will at once begin to exert itself, and, adding effort to effort, patience to patience, and strength to strength, will never cease to develop, and will at last grow divinely strong.

As physically weak people can make themselves strong by careful and patient training, so can people with weak thoughts make themselves strong by exercising themselves in right thinking.

To put away aimlessness and weakness, and to begin to think with purpose, is to enter the ranks of those strong ones who only recognize failure as one of the pathways to attainment, who make all conditions serve them, and who think strongly, attempt fearlessly, and accomplish masterfully.

Having conceived of our purpose, we should mentally mark out a *straight* pathway to its achievement, looking neither to the right nor the left. Doubts and fears should be rigorously excluded; they are dis-

integrating elements which break up the straight line of effort, rendering it crooked, ineffectual, useless. Thoughts of doubt and fear never accomplished anything, and never can. They always lead to failure. Purpose, energy, power to do, and all strong thoughts cease when doubt and fear creep in.

The will to do springs from the knowledge that we *can* do. Doubt and fear are the great enemies of knowledge, and those who encourage them, who do not slay them, thwart themselves at every step.

Those who have conquered doubt and fear have conquered failure. Their every thought is allied with power, and all difficulties are bravely met and wisely overcome. Their purposes are seasonably planted, and they bloom and bring forth fruit which does not fall prematurely to the ground.

Thought allied fearlessly to purpose becomes creative force; those who *know* this are ready to become something higher and stronger than mere bundles of wavering thoughts and fluctuating sensations; those who *do* this—align their thoughts fearlessly

with their purpose—become the conscious and intelligent wielders of their mental powers.

FIVE

Thought as a Factor in Achievement

All that you achieve and all that you fail to achieve is the direct result of your own thoughts. In a justly ordered universe, where loss of equilibrium would mean total destruction, individual responsibility must be absolute. Your weakness and strength, your purity and impurity, are your own, and not anyone else's; they are brought about by yourself, and not by another; and they can only be altered by yourself, never by anyone else. Your condition is also your own, and not anyone else's. Your suffering and your happiness are evolved from within. As you think, so you are; as you continue to think, so you remain.

Stronger people cannot help the weaker unless the weaker are *willing* to be helped, and even then the weaker must become strong of themselves; they must, by their own efforts, develop the strength which they admire in others. Only we ourselves can alter our conditions.

Both oppressors and those who are oppressed are cooperating in ignorance, and, while seeming to afflict each other, are in reality afflicting themselves. A perfect knowledge perceives the action of law in the weakness of the oppressed and the misapplied power of the oppressor; a perfect love, seeing the suffering which both states entail, condemns neither; a perfect compassion embraces both the oppressor and the oppressed.

Those who have conquered weakness, and have put away all selfish thoughts, belong neither to oppressor nor oppressed. They are free.

We can only rise, conquer, and achieve, by lifting up our thoughts. We can only remain weak, and abject, and miserable by refusing to lift up our thoughts.

Before we can achieve anything, even worldly things, we must lift our thoughts above extreme self-indulgence. We do not have to give up *all* selfishness, in order to succeed, but a portion of it must, at least, be given up. If our dominant thoughts are those of indulgence, we can neither think clearly

nor plan methodically; we cannot find and develop our latent resources, and so we fail in any undertaking. Not having commenced to effectively control our thoughts, we are not in a position to control affairs and to adopt serious responsibilities. We are not fit to act independently and stand alone. But we are limited only by the thoughts which we choose.

There can be no progress, no achievement, without a certain degree of sacrifice, and our worldly success will be directly proportional to the degree that we overcome selfish, indulgent thoughts and fix our minds on the development of our plans, and the strengthening of our resolution and self-reliance. And the higher we lift our thoughts, the more upright, righteous, and idealistic we become, the greater will be our success, and the more blessed and enduring will be our achievements.

The universe does not favor the greedy, the dishonest, the vicious, even though on the mere surface it may sometimes appear to do so; it helps the honest, the magnanimous,

the virtuous. All the great teachers of the
ages have declared this in varying forms,
and to prove and know it we have but to
persist in making ourselves more virtuous by
lifting up our thoughts.

Intellectual achievements are the result
of thought consecrated to the search for
knowledge, or for the beautiful and true in
life and nature. Such achievements may be
sometimes connected with vanity and ambi-
tion, but they are not the outcome of those
characteristics, they are the natural out-
growth of long and arduous effort, and of
pure and unselfish thoughts.

Spiritual achievements are the consum-
mation of holy aspirations. Those who live
constantly in the conception of noble and
lofty thoughts, who dwell upon all that is
pure and unselfish, will, as surely as the sun
reaches its zenith and the moon is full, become wise and noble in character, and rise
into a position of influence and blessedness.

Achievement, of whatever kind, is the
crown of effort, the diadem of thought. By the
aid of well-directed thought, resolution, self-

control, and righteousness, we ascend; by the aid of laziness, lack of self-control, and confusion of thought, we descend.

We may rise to high success in the world, and even to lofty altitudes in the spiritual realm, and then descend into weakness and wretchedness by allowing arrogant, selfish, and corrupt thoughts to take possession of us.

Victories attained by right thought can only be maintained by watchfulness. Many give way when success is assured, and rapidly fall back into failure.

All achievements, whether in the business, intellectual, or spiritual world, are the result of definitely directed thought, are governed by the same law and are of the same method; the only difference lies in *the object of attainment*.

Those who would accomplish little must sacrifice little; those who would achieve much must sacrifice much; those who would attain highly must sacrifice greatly.

SIX

Visions
and
Ideals

The dreamers are the saviors of the world. As the visible world is sustained by the invisible, so humanity, through all its trials and mistakes and suffering, is nourished by the beautiful visions of its solitary dreamers.

Humanity cannot forget its dreamers; it cannot let their ideals fade and die. It lives in them; it knows them as the *realities* which it shall one day see and know.

Composer, sculptor, painter, poet, prophet, sage, these are the makers of the afterworld, the architects of heaven. The world is beautiful because they have lived; without them, laboring humanity would perish.

Those who cherish a beautiful vision, a lofty ideal in their hearts, will one day realize it. Columbus cherished a vision of another world, and he discovered it; Copernicus fostered the vision of a multiplicity of worlds

and a wider universe, and he revealed it; Buddha beheld the vision of a spiritual world of stainless beauty and perfect peace, and he entered into it.

Cherish your visions; cherish your ideals; cherish the music that stirs in your heart, the beauty that forms in your mind, the loveliness that drapes your finest thoughts, for out of them will grow all delightful conditions, all heavenly environment; of these, if you remain true to them, your world will at last be built.

To desire is to obtain; to aspire is to achieve. Shall our basest desires receive the fullest measure of gratification, and our purest aspirations starve for lack of sustenance? Such is not the law of the universe; such a condition of things can never obtain. "Ask and you will receive."

Dream lofty dreams, and as you dream, so shall you become. Your vision is the promise of what you shall one day be; your ideal is the prophecy of what you shall at last unveil.

The greatest achievement was at first and for a time a dream. The oak sleeps in the

acorn; the bird waits in the egg; and in the highest vision of the soul a waking angel stirs. Dreams are the seedlings of realities.

Your circumstances may be uncongenial, but they shall not long remain so if you but perceive an ideal and strive to reach it. You cannot travel *within* and stand still *without*.

Here is a young woman, and here is a young man, both hard pressed by poverty and labor; confined long hours in an unhealthy workshop; uneducated, and lacking all the arts of refinement. But they both dream of better things; they think of intelligence, of refinement, of grace and beauty. They conceive of, mentally build up, an ideal condition of life; the vision of a wider liberty and a larger scope takes possession of them; unrest urges them to action, and they utilize all their spare time and means, small though they are, to the development of their latent powers and resources. Very soon their minds have become so altered that the workshop can no longer hold them. It has become so out of harmony with their mentality that it falls

out of their lives as a garment is cast aside, and, with the growth of opportunities which fit the scope of their expanding powers, both of them pass out of it forever.

Years later we see them as full-grown adults. We find them, each in their own unique way, masters of certain forces of the mind which they wield with worldwide influence and almost unequalled power. In their hands they hold the cords of gigantic responsibilities; they speak, and lives are changed; men and women hang upon their words and remold their characters, and, sunlike, they become the fixed and luminous center around which innumerable destinies revolve. They have realized the vision of their youth. They have become one with their ideals.

And you too, youthful reader, will realize the vision—not the idle wish—of your heart, be it base or beautiful, or a mixture of both, for you will always gravitate toward that which you, secretly, most love. Into your hands will be placed the exact results of your own thoughts; you will receive that which you earn, no more, no less.

Whatever your present environment may be, you will fall, remain, or rise with your thoughts, your vision, your ideal. You will become as small as your controlling desire; you will become as great as your dominant aspiration.

In the beautiful words of Stanton Kirkham Davis,

> *"You may be keeping accounts, and presently you shall walk out of the door that for so long has seemed to you the barrier of your ideals, and shall find yourself before an audience—the pen still behind your ear, the inkstains on your fingers—and then and there shall pour out the torrent of your inspiration.*
>
> *"You may be driving sheep, and you shall wander to the city—bucolic and open-mouthed; and you wander under the intrepid guidance of the spirit into the studio of the master, and after a time he shall say, 'I have nothing more to teach you.' And now you have become the master, who did so recently dream of great things while driving sheep. You shall lay down the saw and the plane to take upon yourself the regeneration of the world."*

The thoughtless, the ignorant, and the lazy, seeing only the apparent effects of things and not the things themselves, talk of luck, of fortune, and chance. Seeing some-one grow rich, they say, "How lucky they are!" Observing another become a renowned scholar, they exclaim, "How highly favored they are!" And noting the saintly character and wide influence of others, they remark, "How luck aids them at every turn!"

They do not see the trials and failures and struggles which these men and women have voluntarily encountered in order to gain their experience; they have no knowl-edge of the sacrifices they have made, of the undaunted efforts they have put forth, of the faith they have exercised, that they might overcome the apparently insurmountable, and realize the vision of their heart. They do not know the darkness and the heartaches; they only see the light and joy, and call it "luck"; they do not see the long and arduous journey, but only see the pleasant goal, and call it "good fortune"; they do not understand the process, but only perceive the result, and call it "chance."

In all human affairs there are *efforts,* and there are *results,* and the strength of the effort is the measure of the result. It is not chance. So-called "gifts", powers, material, intellectual, and spiritual possessions are the fruits of effort; they are thoughts completed, objects accomplished, visions realized.

The vision that you glorify in your mind, the ideal that you enthrone in your heart—this you will build your life by, and this you will become.

SEVEN

Serenity

C almness of mind is one of the beautiful
jewels of wisdom. It is the result of long
and patient effort in self-control. Its presence
is an indication of ripened experience, and of
a more than ordinary knowledge of the laws
and operations of thought.

We become calm in the measure that we
understand ourselves as thought-evolved be-
ings, for such knowledge necessitates the
understanding of others as the result of
thought, and as we develop a right understanding, and see more and more clearly the
internal relations of things by the action of
cause and effect, we cease to fuss and fume
and worry and grieve, and remain poised,
steadfast, serene.

People who are calm, having learned
how to govern themselves, know how to
adapt themselves to others; and these others,
in turn, revere the calm people's spiritual

strength, and feel that they can learn from them and rely upon them.

The more tranquil we become, the greater is our success, our influence, our power for good. Even the most ordinary salespeople, for example, will find their business prosperity increase as they develop a greater self-control and equanimity, for people will always prefer to deal with people whose manner is pleasant and steady.

Strong, calm people are always loved and revered. They are like shade-giving trees in a thirsty land, or a sheltering rock in a storm.

Who does not love a tranquil heart, a sweet-tempered, balanced life? It does not matter whether it rains or shines, or what changes come to those possessing these blessings, for they are always sweet, serene, and calm. That exquisite poise of character which we call serenity is the last lesson of our culture; it is the flowering of life, the fruitage of the soul. It is precious as wisdom, and more to be desired than gold—yes, than even fine gold. How insignificant mere money-seeking

looks in comparison with a serene life—a life that dwells in the ocean of truth, beneath the waves, beyond the reach of the tempests, in the eternal calm!

How many people do we know who sour their lives, who ruin all that is sweet and beautiful by explosive tempers, who destroy their poise of character, and make bad blood! It is a question whether the great majority of people do not ruin their lives and mar their happiness by lack of understanding and self-control. How few people we meet in life who are well-balanced, who have that exquisite poise which is characteristic of the finished character!

Yes, humanity surges with uncontrolled anger, is tumultuous with ungoverned grief, is blown about by anxiety and doubt. Only the truly wise, whose thoughts are controlled and purified, make the winds and the storms of the soul obey them.

Tempest-tossed souls, wherever you may be, under whatever conditions you may live, know this: In the ocean of life the isles of blessedness are smiling, and the sunny shore

of your ideal awaits your coming. Keep your hand firmly upon the helm of thought. In the ship of your soul reclines the commanding Master—he does but sleep; wake him. Self-control is strength; right thought is mastery; calmness is power. Say unto your heart, "Peace, be still!"

OTHER BOOKS AND TAPES
FROM
WHATEVER PUBLISHING

We invite you to send for a free copy of our full-color catalog so that you can see our complete selection of books and cassettes. Write or call:

> Whatever Publishing, Inc.
> P.O. Box 13257, Northgate Station
> San Rafael, CA 94913
> (415) 472-2100

ORDER TOLL FREE WITH YOUR VISA/MC
(800) 227-3900
(800) 632-2122 in California

BOOKS

Creative Visualization by Shakti Gawain. This clear and practical guide contains easy-to-use techniques to: feel more relaxed and peaceful, increase your vitality and improve your health, develop your creative talents, create more fulfillment in relationships, reach your career goals, dissolve negative habit patterns, increase your prosperity, and much, much more.

Living in the Light by Shakti Gawain. Shows us a new way of life—becoming a channel for the creative power of the Universe by developing our intuition. Offers both practical and inspirational guidance in expanding our perspective on who we are and what we have the potential to become.

Friends and Lovers—How to Create the Relationships You Want by Marc Allen. An upbeat, knowledgeable, and contemporary guide to living and working with people. Contains a six-step process that is *guaranteed to settle arguments* at home or at work.

Work With Passion—How To Do What You Love For A Living by Nancy Anderson. This highly effective guide will help you master the secrets of finding your niche in life—doing what you love to do and getting paid well for it. *Work With Passion* is filled with inspiring stories of ordinary people who have achieved extraordinary results by following the nine-step program of the author, developed during her years as a highly successful career consultant. This is *the* career book of the 1980's!

Tantra for the West—A Guide to Personal Freedom by Marc Allen. Practical and informative, *Tantra for the West* presents proven principles and techniques to improve the quality of your life in all areas: relationships, sex,

work, money, being alone, creativity, food and drink, meditation and yoga, aging and healing, politics, enlightenment and freedom. "A clear and timely book..."—Marilyn Ferguson.

CASSETTES

As You Think. Marc Allen introduces and then reads his entire, unabridged version of this classic self-improvement book by James Allen. Repeated listening of these powerful, moving words is guaranteed to have a positive effect upon the quality of your life.

Living in the Light. In this powerful hour-long interview, Shakti Gawain reveals the main principles and techniques from her book of the same title, showing us how to connect with our intuition and become a creative channel for personal and planetary transformation.

Stress Reduction and Creative Meditations. Marc Allen guides you through a deeply relaxing, stress-reducing experience on the first side. Side Two contains effective, creative meditations for health, abundance, and fulfilling relationships. Soothing background music by Jon Bernoff.

Creative Visualization. Shakti Gawain guides you through some of the most powerful

and effective meditations and techniques from her book.

Friends and Lovers—How to Create the Relationships You Want*.* In this dynamic cassette companion to his book, Marc Allen gives an interview highlighting the most important ideas and techniques from *Friends and Lovers*. Inner work and core beliefs are stressed.

Anybody Can Write*.* Jean Bryant highlights some of the writing techniques and ideas from her book: trusting yourself, writing without thinking, escape writing, writing with passion, fingerpainting with words.